Never give up. Never give up.

Got to stick to it, got to keep trying. Never give up.

Things may get in your way.

There may be a big delay.

Never give up. Never give up.

Got to stick to it, got to keep trying. Never give up.

Your first try may be a flop,

But be patient and don't stop.

Never give up. Never give up.

Got to stick to it, got to keep trying. Never give up.

Perseverance is what you need.

Try again and you'll succeed.

Never give up. Never give up.

Got to stick to it, got to keep trying.

Never give up.